HBJ TREASURY OF LITERATURE

ACROSS THE FIELDS

SENIOR AUTHORS
ROGER C. FARR
DOROTHY S. STRICKLAND

AUTHORS
RICHARD F. ABRAHAMSON
ELLEN BOOTH CHURCH
BARBARA BOWEN COULTER
MARGARET A. GALLEGO
JUDITH L. IRVIN
KAREN KUTIPER
JUNKO YOKOTA LEWIS
DONNA M. OGLE
TIMOTHY SHANAHAN
PATRICIA SMITH

SENIOR CONSULTANTS
BERNICE E. CULLINAN
W. DORSEY HAMMOND
ASA G. HILLIARD III

CONSULTANTS
ALONZO A. CRIM
ROLANDO R. HINOJOSA-SMITH
LEE BENNETT HOPKINS
ROBERT J. STERNBERG

 HARCOURT BRACE JOVANOVICH, INC.
Orlando   Austin   San Diego   Chicago   Dallas   New York

Printed in the United States of America

ISBN 0-15-301359-1

2 3 4 5 6 7 8 9 10   048   96   95   94   93

Acknowledgments

For permission to reprint copyrighted material, grateful acknowledgment is made to the following sources:

Delacorte Press, a division of Bantam Doubleday Dell Publishing Group, Inc.: Cover illustration from *The Chicken Book* by Garth Williams. Copyright © 1946, 1970 by Garth Williams.

Aileen Fisher: "Baby Chick" from *Runny Days, Sunny Days* by Aileen Fisher. Text copyright © 1958 by Aileen Fisher; text copyright renewed © 1986 by Aileen Fisher.

Greenwillow Books, a division of William Morrow & Company, Inc.: *Across the Stream* by Mirra Ginsburg, illustrated by Nancy Tafuri. Text copyright © 1982 by Mirra Ginsburg; illustrations copyright © 1982 by Nancy Tafuri. Cover illustration by Byron Barton from *Good Morning, Chick* by Mirra Ginsburg. Illustration copyright © 1980 by Byron Barton. *What Game Shall We Play?* by Pat Hutchins. Copyright © 1990 by Pat Hutchins. *I Wish I Could Fly* by Ron Maris. Copyright © 1986 by Ron Maris. Cover illustration by Jose Aruego and Ariane Dewey from *One Duck, Another Duck* by Charlotte Pomerantz. Illustration copyright © 1984 by Jose Aruego and Ariane Dewey. *Flap Your Wings and Try* by Charlotte Pomerantz, illustrated by Nancy Tafuri. Text copyright © 1989 by Charlotte Pomerantz; illustrations copyright © 1989 by Nancy Tafuri.

HarperCollins Publishers: "Wouldn't You?" from *You Read to Me, I'll Read to You* by John Ciardi. Text copyright © 1962 by John Ciardi. "All That Sky" from *Out in the Dark and Daylight* by Aileen Fisher. Text copyright © 1980 by Aileen Fisher. Cover illustration by Crockett Johnson from *The Carrot Seed* by Ruth Krauss. Illustration copyright © 1945 by Crockett Johnson.

Robert B. Luce, Inc.: "Point to the Right" from *Let's Do Fingerplays!* (Retitled: "Where To Look") by Marion F. Grayson. Text copyright © 1962 by Marion F. Grayson.

Macmillan Publishing Company: The Chick and the Duckling by Mirra Ginsburg, illustrated by Jose and Ariane Aruego. Text copyright © 1972 by Mirra Ginsburg; illustrations copyright © 1972 by Jose Aruego.

G. P. Putnam's Sons, a division of the Putnam & Grosset Group: Cover illustration from *Jen the Hen* by Colin and Jacqui Hawkins. Copyright © 1985 by Colin and Jacqui Hawkins.

Handwriting models in this program have been used with permission of the publisher, Zaner-Bloser, Inc., Columbus, OH.

Photograph Credits

6–7 (all), HBJ Photo; 8, HBJ/Britt Runion; 33, HBJ Photo; 40–41, HBJ/Terry Sinclair; 63, SuperStock; 64, HBJ/Britt Runion; 66, HBJ Photo; 89, AllStock; 102, HBJ Photo; 120–121, HBJ/Rich Franco; 122–123, HBJ Photo.

Illustration Credits

Table of Contents Art
Gerald Bustamante, left, 4; Roseanne Litzinger, center, 4, 5; Gerald McDermott, right, 5

Bookshelf Art
Roseanne Litzinger, 6, 7

Unit Opening Patterns
Tracy Sabin

Theme Opening Art
Gerald McDermott, 8, 9; Sue Williams, 64, 65

Selection Art
Pat Hutchins, 10–32; Loretta Krupinski, 34–39; Ron Maris, 40–62; Nancy Tafuri, 66–88; Sylvie Daigneault, 90–101; Jose and Ariane Aruego, 102–119; Nancy Tafuri, 122–140

Dear Reader,

Reading can take you across an open field or all around the world. Open a book and off you go. You can meet the animals in a forest. You can see the gulls at the sea! Where do you think a chick and a duck might live?

Read the stories. Enjoy the poems. You'll find that the animals in this book have wishes and dreams. That's a lot like you and me and people all over the world. Learn about yourself through your animal friends everywhere.

Sincerely,
The Authors

ACROSS·THE·FIELDS

C O N T E N T S

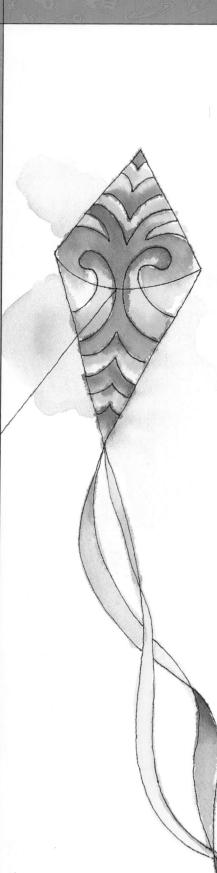

FEATHERED FRIENDS / 64

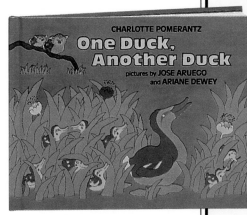

ONE DUCK, ANOTHER DUCK
BY CHARLOTTE POMERANTZ

An owl named Danny goes to the pond with his grandmother. Danny tries to count the ducks. "One duck, another duck," he says. Count the ducks with Danny. AWARD-WINNING AUTHOR

JEN THE HEN
BY COLIN AND JACQUI HAWKINS

Jen the hen is a very clever hen. She writes a letter for Ken and Ben and gives it to Wren. Will Wren be able to find Ken and Ben?

AWARD-WINNING AUTHORS

HBJ LIBRARY BOOKS

GOOD MORNING, CHICK
BY MIRRA GINSBURG

A young chick hatches from his shell. His mother teaches him to eat worms, seeds, and crumbs. The chick tries to learn all kinds of things that he may be too young for. CHILDREN'S CHOICE

THE CHICKEN BOOK
BY GARTH WILLIAMS

Here is a rhyming story about some little chicks. What do chicks like to eat? See if you can guess.

THE CARROT SEED
BY RUTH KRAUSS

A little boy plants a carrot seed. His family tells him, "It won't come up." Do you think the seed will come up? Read the book to find out.

AWARD-WINNING AUTHOR

7

8

PAT HUTCHINS

What Game
Shall We Play?

AWARD-WINNING
AUTHOR/
ILLUSTRATOR

SHARED READING

Duck and Frog went out to play.
"What game shall we play?"
asked Duck.
"I don't know," said Frog.
"Let's go and ask Fox."

11.

So off they went to look for Fox.
Duck looked across the fields,
but he wasn't there.

Frog looked among the tall grass,

13

and there he was.

14

"What game shall we play, Fox?" they asked.
"I don't know," said Fox.
"Let's go and ask Mouse."

So off they went to look for Mouse.
Duck looked over the wall,
but Mouse wasn't there.
Frog looked under the wall,
but she wasn't there, either.

So Fox looked in the wall,

and there she was.

"What game shall we play, Mouse?"
 they asked.
"I don't know," said Mouse.
"Let's go and ask Rabbit."

So off they went to look for Rabbit.
Duck looked near his hole,
Frog looked on top of the hole,
Fox looked around the hole,

and Mouse looked in the hole,

and there he was.

"What game shall we play,
Rabbit?" they asked.
"I don't know," said Rabbit.
"Let's go and ask Squirrel."

So off they went to look for Squirrel.
Duck looked behind the tree,
Frog looked in front of the tree,
Fox looked up to the top of the tree,
Mouse looked under the tree,

and Rabbit looked
through the leaves
of the tree,

and there she was.

"What game shall we play, Squirrel?"
they asked.
"I don't know," said Squirrel.
"Let's find Owl and ask him."

But Owl found them first.
"What game shall we play, Owl?"
they asked.
"Hide and seek," said Owl.

And while Owl closed his eyes,
Duck and Frog hid in the pond,
Fox hid in the long grass,
Mouse hid in the wall,
Rabbit hid in the hole,
and Squirrel hid in the leaves
in the tree.

Then Owl went to look for them.

Where To Look

An action rhyme
by Marion Grayson

Look to the right of me.

Look to the left of me.

Look up above me.

Look down below.

Right, left, up,

And down so slow.

Where Is Thumbkin?

A traditional song

Where is Thumbkin?

Where is Thumbkin?

Here I am.

Here I am.

How are you this morning?

I am fine, thank you.

Walk away.

Walk away.

illustrated by Loretta Krupinski

34

Where is Pointer?

Where is Pointer?

Here I am.

Here I am.

How are you this morning?

I am fine, thank you.

Hop away.

Hop away.

35

Where is tall man?
Where is tall man?
Here I am.
Here I am.
How are you this morning?
I am fine, thank you.
Jump away.
Jump away.

Where is ring man?

Where is ring man?

Here I am.

Here I am.

How are you this morning?

I am fine, thank you.

Run away.

Run away.

SEAFOOD

26

FRESH
COD
$2.50

Where is small man?

Where is small man?

Here I am.

Here I am.

How are you this morning?

I am fine, thank you.

Run away.

Run away.

38

Where are all the men?

Where are all the men?

Here we are.

Here we are.

How are you this morning?

We are fine, thank you.

Run away.

Run away.

39

"Good morning, Bird.

I wish I could fly like you."

CRASH! BANG!
WALLOP! CRUNCH!

"Hello, Frog.
I wish I could dive
like you."

FLOP! PLOP!
SPLUTTER! SPLASH!

"How are you, Squirrel?
I wish I could climb
like you."

WIBBLE! WOBBLE!
WRIGGLE! ROCK!

"Good day, Rabbit.
I wish I could run like you."

PUFF! PANT!
STAGGER! GASP!

"I can't fly like Bird,
I can't dive like Frog,
I can't climb like Squirrel,
I can't run like Rabbit,
but...

"When it rains,
I don't get wet.
I'm **SNUG, WARM,
COZY,** and **DRY!**"

Wouldn't You?

If I

Could go

As high

And low

As the wind

As the wind

As the wind

Can blow—

I'd go!

John Ciardi

WHEATFIELD WITH A LARK (1887)
Vincent van Gogh (1853–1890), Dutch
Rijksmuseum, Amsterdam

FEATHERED FRIENDS

Do you have any feathered friends? Here's your chance to make a few more.

C O N T E N T S

I'm a little baby bird
Wondering how to fly.
See my Grandma in the sky,
Why can't I, can't I?

See my Grandpa in the sky,
Why can't I, can't I?
Mommy whispers, Hushaby,
By and by you'll fly.

72

Daddy sings a lullaby,
By and by and by.

Sister says, Why don't you try?
Flap your wings and try.
So I flap my wings
and try,

And soon I'm in the sky!
Look at me, way up high,
I can fly, can fly!

Below me is a baby bird.
She sees me in the sky.
I can almost hear her sigh,
Why can't I, can't I?

Down,
　　down,
　　　　down, way down I fly
And say, Why don't you try?

I watch her flap her wings
and try,

And soon she's in the sky!
Look at us, way up high,
We can fly, can fly!

85

Below us baby birds call, Why,
Why can't I, can't I?
Hush, we tell them, Hushaby,
You will fly, will fly.

86

You will fly,
by and by,
by and by and by.

All That Sky

by Aileen Fisher

Wouldn't you think
the birds that fly
would lose their way
in *all that sky?*

SIX LITTLE DUCKS

A traditional song

Illustrated by

Sylvie Daigneault

Six little ducks
went swimming one day,
Over the pond and far away.

Mother duck said,
"Quack, quack, quack."
And five little ducks
came swimming right back.

Five little ducks
went swimming one day,
Over the pond and far away.

Mother duck said,
"Quack, quack, quack."
And four little ducks
came swimming right back.

Four little ducks
went swimming one day,
Over the pond and far away.

Mother duck said,
"Quack, quack, quack."
And three little ducks
came swimming right back.

Three little ducks
went swimming one day,
Over the pond and far away.

Mother duck said,
"**Quack, quack, quack.**"
And two little ducks
came swimming right back.

Two little ducks
went swimming one day,
Over the pond and far away.

Mother duck said,
"Quack, quack, quack."
And one little duck
came swimming right back.

One little duck
went swimming one day,
Over the pond and far away.

Mother duck said,
"Quack, quack, quack."
And no little ducks
came swimming right back.

The Chick and the Duckling

Translated from the Russian of V. Suteyev

by Mirra Ginsburg
Pictures by Jose & Ariane Aruego

A Duckling came out of the shell.

"I am out!" he said.

"Me too," said the Chick.

"I am taking a walk,"
said the Duckling.

"Me too," said the Chick.

"I am digging a hole,"
said the Duckling.

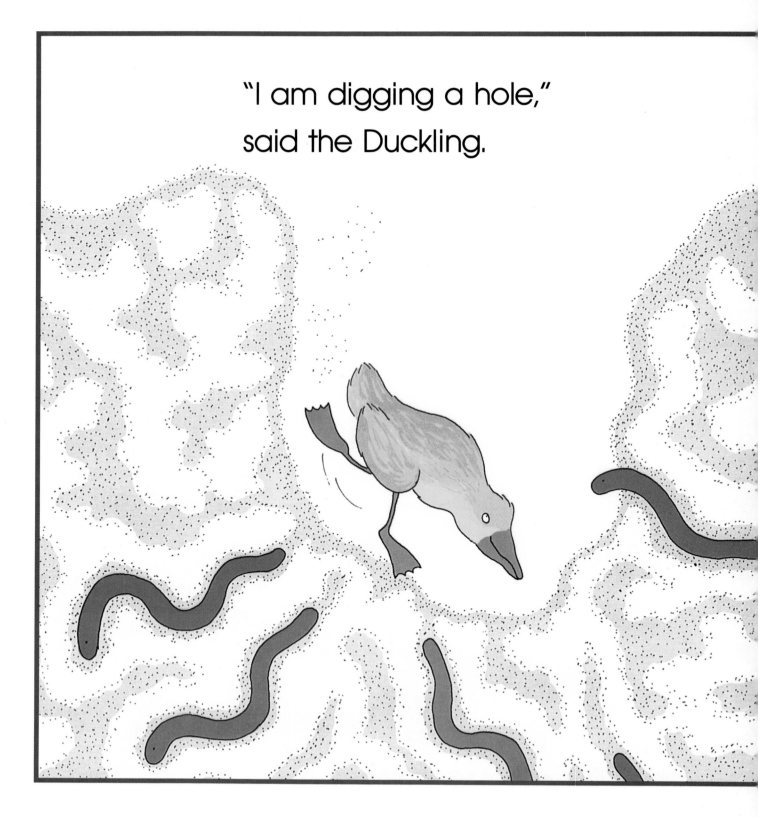

"Me too,"
said the Chick.

"I found a worm,"
said the Duckling.

"Me too,"
said the Chick.

"I caught a butterfly," said the Duckling.

"Me too," said the Chick.

"I am going for a swim,"
said the Duckling.

"I am swimming,"
said the Duckling.

"Me too!"
cried the Chick.

The Duckling pulled
the Chick out.

"I'm going for
another swim,"
said the Duckling.

"Not me,"
said the Chick.

Baby

by Aileen Fisher

Peck

peck

peck

on the warm brown egg.

OUT comes a neck.

OUT comes a leg.

Chick

How
does
a chick
who's not been about,
discover the trick
of how to get out?

ACROSS THE STREAM

BY MIRRA GINSBURG

PICTURES BY NANCY TAFURI

ALA NOTABLE BOOK

AWARD-WINNING ILLUSTRATOR

A hen

and three chicks

had a
bad
dream.

They ran and came

to a
deep,
wide
stream.

131

The hen said, "Cluck, we are in luck.

I see three ducklings

and a duck."

The duck was kind,
she did not mind.

She said, "Quack,
get on my back."

137

They were in luck.
They crossed the stream —

a chick on a duckling,

a chick on a duckling,

a chick on a duckling,

and the hen on the duck.

And what became of

the bad dream?

It was left on the other side of the stream.